THE MILLION DOLLAR KID

Open Secrets Parents Ignore In Raising Rich Kids

AF583235

SAMUEL DIXON

THE MILLION DOLLAR

Open Secrets Parents Ignore In Raising Rich Kids

SAMUEL DIXON

© 2020

The Million Dollar Kid

You are permitted and encouraged to share insights from this book online or in your presentations with credit given to the author and reference made to the book.

CONTENTS

INTRODUCTION

Often, the more money you make, the more you spend; that's why more money doesn't make you rich- assets make you rich.

-Robert Kiyosaki

The subject of money is a sensitive one because; accept it or not, we need money to successfully carry out our plans and live comfortably. Even though the subject of money is on the lips of every one; male and female, young and old, the rich and the poor, not many persons understand how it works; this accounts for why it is misused and sometimes grossly abused. It is no wonder that someone would receive millions of naira and in a few days he would go bankrupt. This simply tells us that managing money is equally as important as making it.

If adults struggle with managing money, how do we expect kids to cope? This is one reason parents need to sit up and develop themselves in the area of financial management so that they would not only improve their financial lives, but also help their kids develop a healthy money culture.

It is one thing to work at earning money and it is another thing entirely to manage the money that has been earned. We must teach our kids how to not just make money, but how to also manage it properly. If kids learn how to make money but are not properly tutored in the art of managing it, they would end up squandering the money.

In this book, we shall evaluate the practical ways to raise wealthy and financially responsible kids who not only understand how money works but who also understand the importance of savings and investment.

Understanding How Money Works 1

Moneyisreallyjustanidea

-Coco Chanel

If you want your kids to turn out well, invest twice as much time with them and half as much money

-Abigail VanBuren

Never spend your money before you have earned it

-Thomas Jefferson

It is true that everyone has an opinion of money, including kids. That is, everyone has his/her own idea of what money is, or should be. Understandably so, whatever definition of money one may hold is largely a function of three key factors:

- What he/she was told about money
- What he/she observed about money
- What he/she has experienced about money

All of these form the basis for one's opinion about money and accounts for why there are differing opinions of what money is, to different people. It is important to note that irrespective of how our ideas or beliefs about money was formed, the way we handle money will ultimately be influenced by what we think of it. If I think that money is made to be spent, I will hardly see a need to save; if however I think that I can use the money to get more money, I will hardly struggle with savings and investments.

It is imperative to teach our kids that **money responds to value**; it is not plucked from a tree. Kids have a rather innocent way of seeing and responding to things. They see you go to work every day and then return with some money, no matter how small. Even when they do not see any physical cash with you, they see you buy a few things on your way back from work and then immediately believe that you probably pick up some money at will from your workplace.

Most often than not, you will notice that when your child craves something, he/she comes to you fully assured that they will get it. You may have also noticed that if or when you are unable to provide what they want or desire, they cry. Some kids even resort to accusing parents of not loving them sufficiently. When you cannot consistently provide your kids with what they demand for, they are often inclined to believe that you do not love them as much as you claim. This is simply because they do not understand how money works, hence the need for enlightenment. If they are able to understand it, they will not only be prepare for the future, but will also be able to decide early enough what value they can create in order to attract money as well reduce a lot of financial burdens on you, their parent(s).

Let your child in on what you do. It is not enough to tell them you go to work; let him/her know what you do and why you are being paid. You didn't just get paid because you left the house; you got paid because you worked for it. This would mean that you possess an ability or have the services which the establishment you work for requires or needs and so they pay you for it. Money is a reward for a job done or a service provided.

Make your kids know that if you were unable to fill in that capacity in the establishment where you work, you would not have been hired in the first place and if you are not hired, you would not be paid and when you are not paid, there will be no money to take care of them. This will help them know that they need to build relevant skills early in life to be able to leverage on opportunities when they come.

If you are self-employed, whether you offer goods or service, you get paid by clients because you are skilled in what you do. Your business would not be successful if you were a bad manager or if you had not developed relevant entrepreneurial skills. In the same vein, if you sell services, let your kids know that you are able to earn because you possess or have acquired relevant skills and it would be good to enumerate or list out the skills which makes you relevant. If you didn't possess or acquire such skills, you would not have earned the money you were paid. The point here is: money responds to value. Whether as an employee or a self-employed person, you are able to make money simply because of the value you bring to the table.

Ask your kids what they can do or what they would love to learn to do so that when they are ready, people can pay them for it. This area of their strength is their money niche. That's the value I'm talking about. Disabuse their minds from the ideology that they are too young to earn. Anyone who is not too young to **spend** money is also not too young to **earn** money. They need to choose a niche they are comfortable with which will enable them to earn money and be very good at it. People are smart in their spending these days. No one wants to waste their hard-earned money on frivolities or things that would not add value to them. If you do not have anything valuable to offer, no one would give you their money. Offering something of value means that you have the solution to a problem. Wealth lies in the ability to proffer solutions to existing or anticipated problems.

REFLECTIONS

Wealth lies in being able to proffer solutions to existing or anticipated problems

The money is in the problem

A Kid's ideology about money would largely be influenced by the information you give them

The Money Chain 2

Never take your eyes off the cash flow because it's the lifeblood of business
-Sir Richard Branson

If I had to run a company on three measures, those measures would be customer satisfaction, employee satisfaction and cash flow
-Jack Welch

You never suffer from a money problem: you always suffer from an idea problem
-Robert H. Schuller

There are seven simple steps that can help your kids identify a niche that they do not just love but one that will bring them money.

Step 1: Identify a problem

The first step to attracting money is to identify a problem. Teach your kids that people are willing to part with their hard-earned money only to the extent that they have a solution to their problems. This is why a smart Entrepreneur will always make a lot of money- he/she sees a solution when others see problems.

Your kid is neither too small to make money nor too young to develop an entrepreneurial mindset. As a matter of fact, when it comes to raising wealthy, financially responsible and influential kids, the development of an entrepreneurial mindset is a solid foundation upon which every other thing stands. If they do not have that mindset, they would be unwilling to venture into it. You can imbibe in them the relevant ideologies that would enable them develop the right mindset by constantly talking to them and also buying them good books and movies on related subject matter. When you inculcate this mindset in them, their eyes will be receptive and open to money making opportunities.

A story was told of an eight-year-old girl who noticed that her friends at school loved ice cream but unfortunately, it wasn't sold in their school. No sooner had they rung the bell that the kids would run outside the gate to buy iced cream. She went home and told her mum who sold ice cream, that her friends at school loved ice cream but that they always had to wait until after school hours to buy it. Her mother who did not understand the girl's point looked on at her confused. Seeing that her mother didn't understand what she was trying to say, she told her mum that she would appreciate it if her mother would make more ice cream so that she could take some to sell at school. Her mother obliged her.

On the first day, she was given only ten sachets of ice cream, the girl came back home and told her mum that many of the kids were not happy because the ice cream was exhausted before it got to them so her mother increased the number of supplies until it became too much for the little girl to take to school alone. The girl's mother had to apply to the school, asking for permission to sell in their school and it was approved.

Now, this was an eight-year-old girl who identified a problem and acted on it. By doing this, she was able to solve a problem and at the same time, raise money for her family. This is further proof that money responds to value.

Step 2: Brainstorm

The brainstorming process involves thinking, evaluating, analyzing and getting relevant information about the problem identified. It is not okay to go into a business, contract or job which you know very little about; you need to ask questions, seek counsel and read relevant materials on the subject matter of the identified problem. This is to ensure that no time or resources would be wasted as a result of little or no progress or sales from the business.

Teach your kids that it is okay to be inquisitive and curious about positive things. The search for knowledge and inquiry into observed natural or unnatural phenomena are the basis for the study of Arts and Science. When they identify a problem, let them get all the information they can garner about that particular problem. It will save them a lot of heartache arising from wrong judgment and failed business investments.

Step 3: Do a survey

King Solomon of the Good Book said: "There is nothing new under the sun". This means that it is possible that the problem the kids would have identified may have also been identified by someone else. It is equally likely that someone could already be doing what your child intends to start-up. Although it may not necessarily be in the same environment and even if it is, there is still a need for a survey.

Doing a survey requires you to ask pertinent questions like:

- Has anyone solved this particular problem?
- Who is the person?
- Where is the person located?
- How was the person able to solve this problem?
- What methods did the person employ?
- Is the person successful at it?
- If no, why?
- What can I do differently?

Honest answers to these questions will go a long way to ensure success in that endeavor as well as ensure proper and adequate planning.

Step 4: Create a solution

After the survey has been done, the child should be encouraged to create a solution to the problem he/she has identified and let that solution be unique and peculiar to him/her alone. This will ensure that even if there are a thousand and one people doing the same thing, there must be something different about his/her own style and pattern.

The crux of the matter is that an entrepreneurial process is not complete if you do not create a solution to the problem identified. The solution can be in the form of a good or service depending on the nature of the problem identified.

Step 5: Advertise

Let people know what you do. That eight-year-old girl would not have sold any of the ice creams if she had locked them up in her bag. She let them know that she had a solution to their problem- they didn't have to wait until the close of school to buy ice cream. So, teach them to talk about their business and be proud of it.

Technology has made a lot of things so easy for us. With just a click, thousands of persons can see and have access to your products or services. The kids must learn to maximize the digital space when it comes to business, in this regard, the internet including the social media like Facebook, Instagram, Twitter, and etcetera.

Step 6: Earn

When the above steps have been articulately and meticulously followed and done, earning becomes easy. The implication is that after your child has been able to identify a problem, done the brainstorming, done a survey, created a solution and advertised it, then he/she can easily make money. The solution he/she has created is the value that people will be willing to give their money for.

Step 7: Expand

In Entrepreneurship, growth is necessary. When you start earning, you do not relax and start spending what you have earned. Instead, while earning one thing is needful. You plan to expand and build on what you already have. It is not okay to be satisfied with what you have because you could be or do more. Expansion means growth and growth means more income. So **expand**.

REFLECTIONS

No child is too small to earn

Inculcating and developing the entrepreneurial mindset in your child is of utmost importance

Money is not plucked, it is earned through acquisition of skills and development of value

3 Assets and Liabilities

It is possible to count the number of seeds in an apple but no one can count the number of apple in the seed.

-Robert Schuller

A seed consumed today may mean the consummation of a forest needed for a shade tomorrow.

-Isaac Ijaopo

If you cannot control yourself, do not try to get rich

-Robert Kiyosaki

Earning is the lowest on the rung of wealth. It is not enough to earn, what you do with what you earn determines if you will build wealth or not. Sustainable wealth cannot be built when you spend all you earn on liabilities. It is important to teach your kids the differences between assets and liabilities.

Naturally speaking, kids are attracted to liabilities **first** before assets. As a matter of fact, their definition of wealth is in the number of cool wristwatches, shoes, clothes and toys that they have and the number of cars their parents drive. There is this pride that comes with having their parents to come pick them up in a beautiful car perhaps from school. That's okay; however, they need to be taught that cars, houses, fancy shoes and clothes should not be bought at the expense of an investment that would have comfortably funded those things.

Kids should be taught self-discipline. If a child can be taught early enough to delay gratifications, there is a huge possibility of the child getting wealthy and retiring early in life. They are not to get biscuit merely because they feel like eating biscuit; are they hungry? Is it really necessary? Is it possible to eat cooked food in place of the biscuit and save that money for something else? Now, you would not expect them to accept your idea of not getting biscuits because kids will always be kids. is is where you need to patiently teach and give them reasons why they could do without the biscuit at that time.

Kids desire to look great at all times whether you can afford it or not. There is a difference between looking rich and being rich. It is true that many people are driven by the desire to look rich. As a result, they spend all they have on liabilities just to create the impression that they are doing well. Sadly, they are not because there is no solid financial plan and investment that will sustain them in the days of scarcity. Kids should be taught that the goal is not to appear rich but to be rich and that it can be achieved if they can delay certain unnecessary gratifications.

They must deal with the desire to impress their

friends or be like someone else who they think is doing well. What would it profit them to get all the shoes, clothes and cars and then retire broke when they should be reaping the fruits of their labor? They must see beyond the present into ten, twenty or more years into the future. Whatever seed of wealth or poverty they sow is exactly what they will reap when the long-anticipated "future" comes. This is why the future must always be their focus at all times. Would they rather have all the fancy liabilities than build systems that will fund these luxuries in the near future?

If you help them lay this foundation, they would not be burdens to their kids in their old age. I believe that as much as possible, kids need to look after their parents in their old age, it is also better for parents to plan their lives very well so that in their old age, they would not be burdens to their kids as is the case with many people now. Many parents forget that their kids have responsibilities to attend to. I am not saying that kids should abandon their parents. No. Every responsible child knows that he or she is obligated to look after his/her parents. Imagine a scenario where your parents are financially stable as a result of proper and early planning, you will know that they can afford whatever they need so when you give them anything, it will not be because they cannot afford it but because of your love for them; both circumstances are different. Your kids can grow to become so wealthy that in their old age, they would not be burdens to their kids who are also saddled with the responsibility of building their own financial future.

Your kids should be taught to prepare for the future early enough. If they plan their retirement at an early, when they are old, they would still be financially capable and comfortable enough to meet their needs.

Assets and Liabilities

Assets bring money to you. Although they may be acquired with money, there is an adequate replacement of whatever was spent in the acquisition, unlike liabilities.

Let's consider Lisa's story. She ran into the sitting room excited. Her mother was surprised because it wasn't so easy to find Lisa excited or even smiling. If she was not writing, then she would be with her calculator or calling an agent to know the price of a plot of land from one area to another. Her mother was sure something was wrong with her seeing that she was unemployed and hardly even had transport fare to go anywhere, talk more of getting a plot of land.

"Mama! I got the job! I got the job! I told you I would!"

Her mother was taken aback, "Are you sure of what you are saying?"

"Of course I am. See the letter"
Her mother could neither read nor write but she took the letter anyway.

So Lisa started work the next day and in 28 days, she got her first paycheck. Without wasting any time, she called one of the agents asking him to show her one of the plots of land. She didn't have all the money but made a deposit. She also promised to make deposits every month until she had completed the payment. Gradually, she was able to buy the plot of land. Lisa being a young lady could have gotten herself all the shoes she wanted but she chose to invest in something more profitable. From Lisa's story, it can be clearly seen that she didn't start planning when she got the job. She started long before she got the job. This teaches that we do not purchase assets when it is convenient for us. Neither do we do so when we have all the money. Little drops of water, they say, make a mighty ocean.

Liabilities, in simple terms, are those things that take money away from you without the potential to replace such money. Liabilities can be fixed or current. **Fixed** liabilities include expenses like; debts, household utensils, generator, cable TV, etcetera. **Current** liabilities, on the other hand, are short term financial obligations due within a year. They are expenses on things like clothing, food, transportation, petrol, rent, electricity and etcetera.

Let us consider the story of Mr John who recently got a job. When he was first called to attend the interview, he was reluctant because he was already too familiar and frustrated with the usual "we'll get back to you". His wife did everything within her powers to convince him before he eventually went for the interview. Even though he had lost hope of ever getting employed, he got the job.

When he got his first salary, he was

overwhelmed; he had never had a lump sum of 300,000 naira. The only thing on his mind was to prove to all those who insulted him when he was still unemployed that he was no longer the broke guy they knew him to be. So Mr John went ahead to get some shoes, clothes and a new phone for himself. He thought he deserved the phone because his friend James used the same phone. And then barely five days into the new month, they were broke again.

When Mr John got his next pay, he told his wife that he would renovate their house to make it classier. His wife reminded him that there would be no need for that seeing that it wasn't even their house but Mr. John would not accept. He went on to paint the house, make new chairs and bought a large television set for the sitting room. As usual, they got broke again just a few days into the new month.

As much as possible, teach your kids to build more assets than liabilities because the more their assets outweigh their liabilities, the more wealth they are building. Liabilities cannot make anyone rich and so if your kids must be financially independent, they must focus on building more assets than acquiring liabilities that would not foot their bills.

I have noticed that most liabilities people spend their hard-earned monies on are things that they could do without. Liabilities only massage your ego but leave you broke. Let their investment fund their luxury. If they do not have an investment, they are tilting towards poverty.

The table below illustrates some examples of assets and liabilities

ASSETS	LIABILITIES
Land	Shoes
Houses	Clothes
Money	Bags
Equipment	Cars

Real Estate	Wristwatches
Stock	Edibles
Shares	Debt

Benefits of having Assets

1. It pays you even when you are not actively working
2. It is a source of income for retirement
3. It helps to secure the future for the kids
4. Investment can lead to entrepreneurship. It doesn't only make the family financially comfortable, it also creates job opportunities and grows or builds wealth
5. It guarantees capital growth for future security
6. It is a source of income to supplement earnings by creating multiple streams of income

▪ REFLECTIONS ▪

▪

Let your investment fund your luxury

▪

Liabilities cannot make you rich

▪

Focus on building assets more than acquiring liabilities

4 Savings and Investment

I make myself rich by making my wants few
-Henry David Thoreau

Do not save what is left after spending but spend what is left after saving
-Warren Buffet

Don't work for money. Make it work for you
-Robert Kiyosaki

Savings and investment are the two major determiners to living financially free. In the first chapter, we talked about what people do to earn. If someone earned all the money in the world but is not disciplined enough to save and invest, that person would be working for nothing.

A child must learn to delay gratification; instead of buying more liabilities, the child should be taught to channel that money into assets. He/she should be taught to save and then invest, depending on the amount he/she has been able to save bearing in mind that it takes money to make more money.

The art of saving is not an outdated habit; as a matter of fact, it is an indispensable tool that every child must learn to utilize early in life. Like most kids think, saving is not only for adults; this is exactly why they need to know what saving is and what they stand to gain when they save against all pressures to spend what they have.

Saving simply means putting aside money you do not intend to spend for future use. According to the *Oxford Advanced Learner's Dictionary*, to save is "to keep some money instead of spending it especially in order to buy a particular thing." This definition points to one fact, "purpose". So we are not just saving because we want to, we save with a purpose in mind. When we have a purpose for doing what we do, it affects how we do what we do. Purpose is key in everything we do including how we manage our money. For instance, a child can decide to start saving in order to get a piece of land or even build a house which he/she intends to lease out. That is a definite purpose. Successful saving requires that one has a purpose for saving. If I save with no purpose in mind, it is possible that I would channel that money into something less productive because there was no goal or purpose for saving from the outset.

I have heard many people say they are saving for the rainy days. This is not good enough because you do not save for the rainy days alone; you save for the future. If you teach your child to save for the rainy day, be sure that he/she is bound to spend that money because rainy days will definitely come. I am talking about saving for the future; saving to acquire assets that would bring a chain of cash flow. If your child believes that the reason we save is to prepare for the rainy day, he/she will end up spending it and that means they have nothing for the future.

Saving for the rainy day is not a bad idea but it is best when they are saving for the future as well. Saving both for the rainy day and the future, secures the future because when the rainy day comes, they would not be tempted to attend to its needs from the future savings. So instead of saving for the rainy day alone, please let them save for the future as well.

It is important to know that what makes the difference between the rich and the poor is that the rich save first and then spend from their leftovers while the poor spend first and save from the leftovers. The poor only save after they have satisfied all their wants. This attitude towards money will only render one poor.

Robert Kiyosaki, in his book *Rich dad, Poor Dad,* encourages the principle of *pay yourself first.* This means that when they get paid for a job done, they do not begin with clearing their debts or even acquiring liabilities for themselves. No, they must take out a percentage from the money and save it, thereafter; they could attend to other needs. Except they do this, they risk being poor.

How to Save

In the previous chapter, we talked about assets and liabilities and we listed out some assets that could be acquired. Now, your child may not be able to afford a piece of land but the most important thing is that the child is saving up and as time goes by, his savings increases, giving him an advantage.

Saving does not totally deny one the opportunity of taking care of one's self. By encouraging your kids to save, you need to make them know that it does not mean they have to look tattered or go hungry in order to invest, no. this is why it is encouraged that only a percentage of one's income should be saved. For instance, a child who earns ₦1,000 is encouraged to save at least 10-30% of what he/she earns. This means that he/she would be saving 100 to 300 naira as often as he/she gets ₦1000. The rest of the money is left for him to do other things with it.

Let's say he/she earns ₦1,000 on a monthly basis and then he/she saves ₦300.

₦300×12 months = ₦3,600

₦3,600×5 years =₦ 18,000.

Now, what if your child earns ₦1,000 bi-weekly (twice a week) and saves 30% of his income? That means he would be saving ₦600 every month if he saves up to 30% of his income.

₦600×12 months =₦7,200

₦7200×5 years = ₦36,000

The illustration above is just an instance. Your

child's savings could be more but please try to ensure it is not less. I have met parents who save for their kids; they put money into the savings account as regularly as they have agreed to. This is a good step and should be encouraged but while you are doing that, the child has to be trained to learn to save for himself, otherwise, when he finally has access to the money you have saved over the years for him, he would squander it. You can inculcate the habit of saving in him by getting him involved and making him put in a particular amount of money every month. This teaches him responsibility and he learns commitment alongside his savings skills. Let him know that his savings could be more but that the amount you have agreed to put in with him should not drop, but should rather increase.

Let your child know that as his income increases, his/her savings should also increase. Increment of income does not mean one should increase his/her standard of living. Rather, one should increase his/her savings and continue to live within his/her means. When the saved money is mature enough to get an asset, the child should proceed with it. Money attracts more money in the world of investment so the more the savings, the more returns your child would get.

Sources of Income for your Child

You might be wondering how your child would earn. There are many ways your child can get money. Did you know that you could put your child on salary?

The part of the world where I come from, most parents believe that it is morally wrong to pay a child for doing "what he should do", after all, "I pay his fees and meet his needs". See, there is absolutely nothing wrong with paying your child. You could put your child on a payroll every month and give him responsibilities. For instance, he is to wash the toilet, do the dishes and sweep a part of the house, if the house is too large for him. And when he does that, you could decide to pay him something meager. By doing that, you are training him to be responsible and to a large extent, you would be teaching him how money works. When you pay your child for doing certain house chores, you are simply telling him that money responds to value, just as we mentioned in the first chapter. So, you can actually pay your child. Doing that doesn't mean you are spoiling him; rather, you are simply teaching him a valuable lesson.

A child could also earn through **Tipping**. A member of the family or even a family friend could visit and then give him some money to buy whatever he pleases. Let your child know that he should also save a percentage of that money irrespective of how small it is. By doing this, you would be training and helping him imbibe the principle of saving.

A person who saves understands that there is a

future. We do not save simply because we have so much; we save because we want to adequately prepare for tomorrow.

To invest, on the other hand, is "to buy property or acquire shares in a company or an establishment and to put your money into any venture that brings returns, etc. in the hope of making a profit."

Methods of Saving

There are several methods of saving used by adults which can equally be utilized by kids. We shall consider two common methods.

1. **Banking**:

These days, there are bank savings accounts for kids. If your child is "techy" and familiar with how smart phones work, you can teach him to always credit his savings account using a mobile app. I mean, kids of this generation are all over the social media. Why not use the same platforms to show him how he/she can save so that he will get familiar with and begin to utilize it?

2. Traditional Saving Boxes (Piggy Bank)

If on the other hand your child is not so "techy" or you would not want to expose him to the digital space so soon, then you could get him a piggy bank. A piggy bank is simply a saving box having a small hole where your child can throw in money.

There are two popular types of piggy banks: the one with a key and the one without a key. Now the saving box without a key is structured in a way that your child would not be able to access the money except the box is broken. Here is my advice: let your child save for a period of one year, then you can have the box opened, and the money counted and deposited into the bank for him. That way, the money would not have to stay so long in the box. Then repair the old one or make a new one for him.

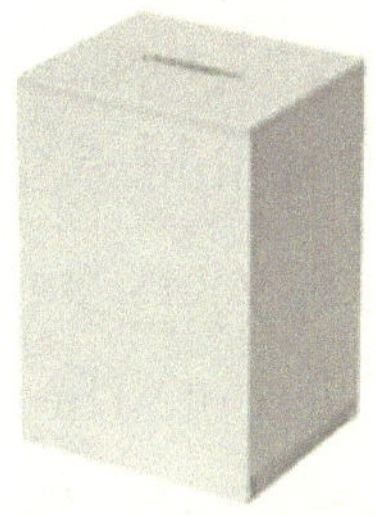

Piggy Bank without a key

The second type of traditional saving box is the one that has a key. Just like the first box, it has a small hole where your child can throw in money but this box doesn't have to be broken for that to happen. All you have to do is break open the padlock or the key without spoiling the bank itself.

Usually, this kind of box is locked and the key, thrown away so that no one would be able to access the money in it.

Piggy Bank with a key

The use of the piggy bank would not work without consistency. Your child would not be able to save up to 96,000 in 8 years as we calculated above if he is not consistent. There is nothing magical about it. Let your child know that consistency is a key factor. If he/she is able to save consistently for 5-10 years, you would have successfully developed and inculcated the saving culture in them.

Benefits of Saving

1. It helps prepare the child for the future
2. Builds a decent financial culture in your child
3. Helps to avoid financial pressures
4. Gives financial freedom
5. Helps prepare for retirement
6. There is an opportunity to earn interest
7. It creates a cycle of wealth
8. It enables the child to learn the principle of financial discipline
9. It enables the child to acquire investment

capabilities

10. It develops the value of consistency in the child.

Investment

The essence of saving basically is not to pile up money in a piggy bank or in an actual financial institution. The essence of saving is to gather enough money to purchase goods, properties or services which would be used in the future to create wealth. This is what we mean by investment. Investing your money is the easiest way to multiply it.

Your savings alone would not make you as wealthy as you desire to be. That is because you need a system that would multiply what you have already. Wealth is built from the multiplication of one's resources. So teach your child to work towards investing his money.

According to Pastor Wisdom Osiri, there are

two types of income; Earned income and passive income. As the name implies, earned income is gotten from the rendering of your physical strength and labor or the provision of physical goods or services. While passive income is gotten from investment in which your money works for you without you having to lift a finger.

The areas of investment available to adults that can be applicable to kids have been listed in the previous chapter under assets and liabilities.

REFLECTIONS

The best time to teach your kids about saving is when they are still kids

Nothing secures the financial future of your child like saving does

It takes a lot of discipline to save
Money wasted or spent is gone forever

Monetary Terminologies

5

Never spend everything you get. It is foolishness.... The amount you got in the first place is irrelevant. What you cannot cover with your present income is not your level. Life is lived in phases. Enjoy your phase per time.

-Pastor Wisdom Osiri

Too many people spend money they earned to buy things they don't want to impress people they don't like

-Will Rogers

Wealth consists not in having great possessions, but in having few wants

-Epictetus

Income

Income is a financial term that represents all the monies that come in or that accrues to a person or an organization. It is the money earned from work, investment or business. All money earned is referred to as income irrespective of how meager or huge it may be.

For the sake of accountability, every income must be properly recorded. Your child should learn to take note of how much he is paid/given and for what purpose he was given the money. For instance, below is an income record of an 8 year old David for the month of December.

S/N	INCOME	SOURCE/PURPOSE	DATE
1	300	Uncle Tammy/TIP	21/12/2019
2	1000	Dad/Salary for December	30/12/2019

The above is a typical income record. We can see that Uncle Tammy tipped David the sum of 300 naira while he got ₦1000 as salary from his father probably for doing the dishes and cleaning his room.

Keeping a record of one's income will help him know how much in total he was able to make or get in a particular month. When this is done properly, it would help him measure his financial progress not only on monthly or quarterly basis but also on an annual or yearly basis.

Your child's expenses should be a percentage of his income and should usually not be higher than 50% of what he has earned in the month. He should be taught that his income must go beyond meeting basic needs. Imperatively, his expenses should not be greater than his income nor should it be higher than what he saves. This is the essence of taking records. Expending more than is earned is a call for poverty. For example, if your child earns ₦2,000 on a monthly basis, he should save at least 60% of his income and then use the remaining 40% to meet his basic needs. Savings should be more because it has the potential to create wealth and acquire assets that would fund whatever luxury your child may seek in the future.

Expenses

Expenses are the things we spend money on. After we earn (income), whatever we use that money to purchase is called an expense. If what we spend money on are not assets, then it is likely that we have spent on liabilities.

The rate of your child's expenses should be controlled and monitored closely otherwise he/she may be tilting towards indebtedness or towards operating a deficit budget. As a matter of fact, expenses are planned based on one's income. Your child should not list out items worth ₦10,000 if his earning is just ₦3,000, where would the other ₦7,000 come from? Now, this is not to say that your child should fend for himself, no. we are talking about raising wealthy and influential kids who know how money works and understand the basic and underlying principles that govern the making and spending of money.

Now, the essence of paying your child on a monthly or weekly basis as you may deem fit is to make him financially responsible. This also implies that if he is earning, he would have to be taught to take care of certain personal needs from his earnings. And of course such needs have to be menial or meager depending on his age and the mount he earns, bearing in mind that you are only trying to teach him financial intelligence and management. He has to be taught that for every time he gets paid or tipped, he is to set aside a certain percentage usually not lower than 60% as savings whilst spending the remaining 40% on his personal needs as planned since the bulk of the expenses for his welfare and upkeep are on you, his parent. This requires a whole level of discipline. Discipline is a major value or trait that should be imparted to your child. Absence of this trait would result in gross mismanagement of resources or may result in your child tending towards a prodigal lifestyle. You can instill financial discipline in your child by teaching him/her to be frugal by delaying gratification and teaching them to learn to live within their means. They have to be taught to evaluate whether or not what they desire to have is something they cannot comfortably purchase or acquire from what they have left after saving, and if not then they must wait and save for it if it is something that they need desperately.

The same way we are careful to take note of our income, there is a need to also keep a track of one's expenses for the sake of accountability. Below is a table showing David's expenses as well.

S/N	EXPENSES	PURPOSE	DATE
1.	₦50	Biscuit	23/12/2019
2.	₦150	A pair of fancy socks	27/12/2019

It is clear from the above table that David is trying to keep record of his expenses. In December of 2019, he made a total of ₦1,300 and spent only ₦200. He didn't have to spend so much because his father took care of his needs. The implication is that he obviously saved ₦1,100 in the month of December which is way above 60% of what he should have saved if he followed the original plan on the exact percentage to save monthly. Even if he had many other things to buy, he must not be permitted to expend beyond 60% of his income.

Debt

Debt is the sum of money that someone owes. In a situation where David decides to buy a toy car worth ₦2,500 when all he has is ₦1,100 as a result of his previous expenses, if he does not discipline himself to delay that gratification, he would be forced to borrow an extra ₦1,400 just to meet up an expense that is higher than what he earns in a month.

Assuming he proceeds to borrow the money, he would be in debt of ₦1,400. As we know, he earns only ₦1,000 as salary from his dad. So as soon as he is paid at the end of the month, he has absolutely nothing to save because he would have to clear his debt by depositing a sum of ₦1,000 which he had just received leaving a balance of ₦400. And assuming David wasn't so lucky to get a tip from anyone in January, he would have to wait until February to be able to pay his outstanding debt of ₦400. Implying that he would not be able to get anything for himself in the new month because ₦400 is 40% of his monthly allowance of ₦1000 and since he has to save up to at least 60% of his income he would be left with the ₦600 savings.

From the above, it is obvious that David used up his savings for the month of December, his salary for January and would also need up to ₦400 from his salary in February if he doesn't get a tip worth that much within the two months. By the singular action of insisting on getting a toy car he could not afford at the moment, he had cheated himself of two months savings and even used up 10% from his salary for

February.

What if he had delayed or even gotten over the urge to get the toy car? Here's what he would have:

₦1,100+₦600 = ₦1,700

600 naira being 60% of his savings for January and if he added his saving for February he would have ₦2,300 but that would be impossible because he had eaten into the future. Kids should be taught to avoid debt, unless it is absolutely necessary.

There are basically two types of debt. Good and bad debt. Good debts are debts taken to purchase assets that would bring in money, enough to pay up the debts and still leave the owner with extra. There is a need for proper investigation before your child would venture into such risk.

Bad debt, on the other hand is like what David

did. Borrowing from his friend to purchase a toy car that would not bring cash inflow, but would rather make him spend from the future funds. This must be totally avoided.

A person who owes is called a debtor and I doubt if anyone would love to be addressed that way.

Budgeting

Budgeting is the act or process of documenting anticipated income and expenditure within a certain period of time and may vary among individuals. Budgeting is so important because it curbs unnecessary expenditures and gives direction to someone on how their money should be spent. If there is no planned budget, the individual is bound to throw in money to anything that comes his way. When there is a budget however, the individual is careful on how money is spent.

Every child should be taught budgeting. Budgeting could be daily, weekly, monthly, quarterly or yearly depending on those involved. A child may not be able to do a yearly budgeting but he/she can do monthly budgeting. He/she should list out the income they expect and the possible expenditures that could emanate from it, not forgetting the 60% benchmark that should be reserved as savings.

In budgeting, there should be a difference between needs and wants. Below is an example of what budgeting looks like:

INCOME	Amount(₦)	EXPENDITURE	Amount (₦)
Salary	1,000	NEEDS: Storybook Pencil	 50 30
Tips	-------	Total	80
		WANTS: Sweets Chewing gum	 10 10
		Balance after needs & wants	80

This budget will guide the child to not exceed his spending limit for the month and even if he does exceed the expenditure limit, he would still have extra because his savings for the month is 60% of 1,000 naira. This does not in any way mean that the child is not encouraged to save beyond the stipulated percentage.

Differences between Needs and Wants

The difference between needs and wants is that needs are those things we cannot do without and which are essential for our survival and comfort and includes amongst other things; food, clothing, shelter, education, access to healthcare, e .t. c. While wants are those things we desire to have but which we can do without because they are not necessities of life. They are very much optional and include among other things; exotic wrist watches, expensive phones, trending wears including shoes, clothes and bags, etc.

Needs and wants are relative concepts because in life, someone's need may be another person's want. Needs and wants differ from person to person. Kids should discipline themselves and deal with the urge to compare themselves with other people. They must be taught to know that needs are more important than wants. Teach them to always evaluate what they desire to get, and ascertain whether it is a need or a want? Can they survive without it? Will it bring money to their table or take from it leaving them completely broke? Their ability to provide positive responses and answers to these questions would determine whether or not they should proceed with the expense.

Benefits of Budgeting

1. It gives vision, clarity and purpose to your child's money
2. It curbs unnecessary expenditures
3. It is specific

4. It demands thorough thinking and teaches your child the ability to brainstorm
5. It exposes selfish interests and inordinate ambition
6. It opens one's eyes to possibilities to earn and invest
7. It checkmates impulsive buying and disciplines expenditure

REFLECTIONS

Income is simply money that comes in

Expenditure is money that goes out

Budgeting is planning your income and expenses for productivity

Debt is borrowing money from someone else to purchase what you cannot afford for yourself

Debt rubs you of your future savings and expenses

Needs describes things you cannot do without
Wants describes things you can do without.

6 The Entitlement Mentality

Man is not, by nature, deserving of all that he wants. When we think that we are automatically entitled to something that is when we start walking all over others to get it
-Chris Jani

It is easy, when you are young, to believe that what you desire is no less than what you deserve, to assume that if you want something badly enough, it is your God-given right to have it.
-Jon Krakauer

What separates privilege from entitlement is gratitude
-Brene Brown

You cannot help people permanently by doing for them, what they could and should do for themselves
- Abraham Lincoln

Majority of the business tycoons we celebrate today did not start out smoothly. Many of them had to go through so many terrible experiences which forced them into thinking and brainstorming on what they could do to raise money for themselves and to enable them fend for those who may be looking up to them like siblings and other family members. Some of them were forced to think because they lost their jobs, while others were forced to do so because they lost their parents at a tender age leaving them without someone to fend for or take care of them. Many others came from families where they could barely feed themselves. These ugly situations and other similar or peculiar circumstances pushed them into discovering, unleashing and maximizing their potentials.

A good number of these people having passed through such situations had vowed to never let their kids go through the adversities they went through in life. As a result, they do everything within their power to make their kids comfortable by providing them with all they need and ask for. They believe that they are helping their kids live a better life but in reality, they are denying the kids the privilege and opportunity of an experience they would need in life.

Whether we like it or not, adversity makes us. There are capacities we develop when we go through certain seemingly ugly experiences. Denying your kids the "opportunity" to experience what the large society and indeed the world feels like would be doing them harm rather than good. Parents who treat their kids like this inadvertently set them up for failures and struggles even though they do not intend to do so because really, when they are faced with certain challenges, they stand a risk to be at loss as to what to do and may eventually mess up. They may have all the money they need but they would not have developed virtues, stamina, experiences and the requisite capacity that would enable them sustain the wealth that has been bequeathed to them by their parents. They feel they are entitled to whatever they ask for or want and are therefore unwilling to work to make or earn a living for themselves.

The entitlement mentality is a state of mind where privileges are considered as rights. As a result, those who are concerned or involved feel deserving of them. This mentality is characterized by arrogance, lack of appreciation, irresponsibility, dependency and ignorance. A good number of present day millionaires are self-made. This means that the wealth they have acquired was by their own efforts and was not bequeathed to them by their parents. They worked for it. If these people do not teach their kids to make money or if they make no effort to help them understand how money works, they would end up committing all they have toiled and labored for into the hands of kids who have no idea whatsoever how the wealth came about or how to manage it. Any wealth that is ill-managed will lead to poverty. Sometimes people do not get poor because they do not make money, no. In some instances, people actually make so much money, but drift into poverty because they lack the proper and adequate management skills necessary to sustain the wealth they have managed to acquire.

Managing money is not as easy as making it. In fact, if making money involves or requires 30% work, managing the money will require 70% more work. This is why it is difficult to maintain generational wealth because succeeding generations have not been adequately or sufficiently trained to do so. Robert Kiyosaki gives an instance of lottery winners who go broke soon after winning millions. According to him, usually, these people are supposed to leverage on their wins to build wealth, instead, they will squander it. If self-discipline and financial management is not part of a child's makeup or upbringing, he would squander whatever wealth is bequeathed to him by his parents and still go about demanding privileges as rights. Entitlement mentality is bad and must be discouraged.

One of the things that are likely to happen when your kids have no idea how money works is that they will feel entitled to everything. This is why some kids would go to the extent of crying and where possible fighting, just to have something that originally does not belong to them; many times without even the slightest effort to request or plead for it. This is wrong and should be adequately addressed.

Going by what we have discussed from chapter one to three of this book, it would be rare for any child who understands how money works to go about with an entitlement mentality. A child who really understands the concept of money would be too responsible to demand anything and even if he/she has to, it would be done politely, with an understanding that the person from whom they are placing such demands reserves the right either to oblige or turn down their requests.

From the foregoing, this entitlement mentality is mainly manifested by kids from rich homes. This is because they have almost everything at their beck and call so they grow up with the mindset that they should be given whatever they desire or ask for. The child from a poor home hardly feels entitled to anything. Instead, he/she feels not deserving of them because they haven't been exposed to and do not have access to certain luxuries in life.

The best time to train your kids not to feel entitled to anything is while they are still kids. Entitlement mentality in kids can be dealt with in several ways. Some of the ways of getting it right includes:

1. **Teach them manners**

Let your kids be taught to always say "please", "thank you" and "I'm sorry". When they learn to use these words, it will help them. Those words or clauses have been described as the magic words and are the three most powerful words. When your child says thank you, he is acknowledging that whatever was given to or done for him/her was not a right but a privilege. When kids say I'm sorry, they acknowledge that they have done wrong and it takes humility to apologize. Same goes for the last word "please". By saying please, the child realizes that the person from whom he needs a favor reserves the right either to refuse or accept his request.

2. **Engage your kids by assigning them domestic responsibilities**

Irrespective of how wealthy you are, please assign responsibilities to your kids. You would be doing them great harm if you refuse them from carrying out tasks at home. Let them do the dishes, wash their clothes, clean their rooms, and do other menial tasks depending on their age and capacity. Please do not leave all the jobs to the maids or other servants.

3. Teach your kids to respect everyone, including the maids

Every parent must learn emotional intelligence. It is no longer an option but a necessity. No matter how angry or upset you are, please do not disrespect anyone in front of your kids, especially the maids. Kids learn primarily by imitation. When they see you treat the maid with respect, they would follow suit and it would rub-off on their relationship with other older persons. If however you disrespect the maids and everyone else in front of them, they would also do the same.

We had said at the beginning of this book that kids should be taught to love and honour everyone. It would be difficult to do so if their first role models, their parents, did otherwise. Help your kids develop a sense of responsibility by being responsible.

4. Discipline your kids when they err

When you give your kids responsibilities and they carry them out as you instructed, do well to appreciate them. If however they fail, do not hesitate or fail to discipline them in love. When you constantly make excuses for their disobedience, you are strengthening and reinforcing their bad habits. By disciplining them, you are simply teaching them a valuable lesson that life is full of responsibilities and any failure in carrying out such responsibilities comes with stiff penalties resulting in suffering for the negligence or disobedience.

REFLECTIONS

Entitlement mentality can deny your kids of a great many opportunities

Entitlement mentality gives a wrong impression of someone's personality

Teach your kids to honour and respect everyone irrespective of their status or background

7 Kids and Early Socialization

The richest people in the world look for and build networks, everyone else looks for work
-Robert Kiyosaki

Your network is your net worth
- Porter Gale

Know where you want to go and make sure the right people know about it
- Meredith Mahoney

No one succeeds in isolation and no one fails in isolation. Jude Ogu, the Principal to one of the fastest growing secondary schools in the city of Port Harcourt, has a famous quote boldly written at the entrance to the school: "when a student fails, he does not fail alone. He fails with his parents, he fails with his teachers and he fails with all those who failed to do their duties". Any man who says he is self-made is either ignorant or selfish because he would be sidelining those who played vital roles on his way up. His parents would have sent him to school and laid the foundation for him to meet at school his teachers who would have taught him virtues and disciplined him when he erred. What about the friends from whom he would have sought counsel when he was probably at the crossroads?

Life is largely about networking. We need people and people need us. Let your child know that no matter how wealthy he thinks his father or mother may be, he still needs people. He must not glory in his parent's wealth to the extent or point that he would bully or maltreat people; for that would amount to shooting himself in the leg. A wise saying goes thus, "be nice to people you meet on your way up because you will meet them on your way down".

A story was told of a boy who came from a rich home. He insulted a fellow kid because the poor kid's father could not afford a good leather sandal for school. The rich kid's father got to know of his son's attitude at school simply because of the luxury he was privileged to access as a result of his father's status. So the man withdrew all the fancy sandals he wore to school and bought for him, exactly what the poor boy wore to school. The father said he did that to teach his son a lesson. We can only imagine how humble that young boy would have become.

Every parent is obligated to teach their kids to respect **everyone** irrespective of their gender, tribe or race, religious or political affiliation and financial status; everyone must be treated right no matter who they are or what they have because we all need people to succeed in life. Truly, if they are patient enough, they would realize that they could learn a thing or two from people who they may consider to be irrelevant or who they think have little if not nothing to offer because everyone actually has something to offer no matter how poorly we may think of them or how bad we may think they are. Your child's ability to relate with different kinds of people will be of great advantage to him/her in the future when he would have to work with different kinds of people from different backgrounds or walks of life and may even have to carry out certain projects with people he never bargained to work with. That's the reality of life. If he didn't learn the art early enough, he would struggle to cope when he eventually finds himself in such circumstances.

Raising wealthy and influential kids does not only entail being financially rich or stable. A wealthy and influential kid must also be rich socially. A wealthy man who has no trustworthy friends or people he could call or depend on in times of distress is socially poor and deficient in relationships. As you teach your child to save and invest, also teach him to consciously invest in building good relationships. As you can see, it is one thing to have friends and an entirely different thing to have a good relationship as well as profitable friendship.

The Power of Right Association

At the beginning of this chapter, I talked about grooming your child to value everyone and accept them the way they are. That is totally valid. However, the child must also learn that accepting everyone the way they are is not the same thing as being friends with all of them. Everyone cannot be his/her friends. Your child has to learn to love everyone but to choose his friends.

A friend is someone who shares similar values with you. From the crowd, there will stand out one or two persons who will share similar values with your child. From 6 years upwards, the child would have come to understand certain basic values and must be able to identify those who share the same values as him; those are his potential friends.

One of the fastest ways to crumble all you have taught your child and every lesson and knowledge he has acquired about wealth creation and management is for him to associate with those who think or have a contrary view to what he has been taught. Friends tend to have a great influence on your child. This is exactly why children tend to ask certain questions once they return from hanging out with their friends. This is one reason you must ensure that they only hangout with the right set of friends.

Here is what a good friend would do:

- Make learning easier for your child
- Teach him more values which he also learnt at home
- Confirm or help reinforce all you have taught him at home

- Encourage him to pursue his dreams
- Speak the truth to him when he seems to be deviating
- Pray for and with him
- Stand up for and support him where necessary

Choose your Child's Friends

As much as your child reserves the right and gets the opportunity to make his own choices, especially in relation to friendship, you have the role of looking out for those he would eventually introduce to you as his friends. Give your child the freedom to bring his friends home so that you can have the opportunity to observe them and then decide if you want your child to proceed in friendship with such persons.

If however you find anyone among them who you either do not agree with or are not comfortable with, here's what you could do:

- Ask yourself why you do not like the child. This would enable you to be clear headed and not make a hasty decision that could spoil or mare the chances of your child getting the value from such associations either immediately or in the future as the case may be.

- Engage the child in a discussion. Ask him pertinent questions especially in relation to values. Take note that some of these kids may not have enlightened parents but have the potential to learn from you. As long as they are willing to learn, you may need to invest in that child for the sake of your own kid.

- If after asking relevant questions you discover or are convinced that the child will be a wrong influence on your child, please do not be rude to the child. Still maintain a loving, polite and calm attitude towards the child until he has gone then you can call your child and inquire from him what his opinion of the friend may be and why he feels he should be friends with him/her? Find out how they became friends and other relevant details about the persons parents and family background.

At this point, you would have become convinced whether the friendship should continue or not. If not, then you must lovingly but sternly instruct your child to stay away from such friends and tell him why it is necessary to do so. You need to be careful while doing this so that you do not send the wrong signal or message. Your child must be taught that he is free to love everyone but that he must be careful in choosing his friends and the people who do not share or respect the values he holds to be true should not be his "friends".

REFLECTIONS

Teach your child to:

Accept people the way they are

Value and respect people

Choose his friends wisely

8 Skill Development at an Early Age

Schooling doesn't assure employment but skill does
- Amit Kalantri

A gap in skills and abilities reveal a golden opportunity
- Anonymous

Skills make you rich. Not theories
Robert Kiyosaki

The best time to impact any skill on your child is while they are young. The mind of a child is like a blank slate where you can write whatever you desire and it would stay with them. It is more difficult to teach them certain things when they are older so if you do not teach them what they should learn, someone else would teach them what they shouldn't and trust me, it is more difficult to "unteach" what has been taught than to teach what hasn't been taught.

In our present day economy, it is not enough to have just one source of income. A paid job is good but it is even better if apart from the regular 9-5, your child has skills that fetch him money. Depending on only one source of income is not enough to build the kind of wealth anyone would wish for. As a matter of fact, wealth is easier to build when resources flow from different directions and meet at a central point. The man who uses a bucket to fetch water will have his drum filled up long before the one using a cup.

Look at this instance, a man who works 9-5 would hardly be able to work in more than two places. This would mean that his only hope of building more sources of income for himself would be to acquire relevant skills that would fetch him the needed money. I know a family whose six year old child can comfortably play the keyboard while their 8 year old daughter can drum beautifully. I was amazed at first until I got to speak with their parents. I was told that they exposed them to the musical instrument from the ages of 3 and 4 respectively. They purchased a drum set and a keyboard and then employed a teacher who came to the house on weekends to teach the kids. Many parents make the mistake of thinking that their kids are too young to learn or acquire a skill. The best time to teach your kids anything is while they are still kids. Give them the materials to play with until they get accustomed to it or eventually settle for the one they are either more comfortable with or are better suited for or efficient with.

Many teenagers gain admission into the university without a skill and as a result are largely dependent on their parents for everything. Many of them end up with the wrong set of people because of pressure from their friends. If these teenagers had a good foundation from home, especially in relation to building wealth and skill development, they would probably be too busy with important things to fall or become prey in the hands of the wrong people. Some of these teenagers and even adults engage in wrong activities because they need money but these are things that they would have comfortably acquired for themselves if they possessed the relevant skills that should have enabled them to do so. Even if your kids are all grown up now, it is not too late to help them acquire a skill. Please do your kids the favour of pushing them to acquire skills early enough. It is better late than never.

Some of the skills your kids can acquire are:

1. Graphic designing
2. Drawing/painting
3. Writing
4. Acting
5. Coding
6. Piano or keyboard playing
7. Confectioneries
8. Ballet
9. Hair making and etcetera.

REFLECTIONS

Kids have a guaranteed chance to learn whatever they wish to

Before the age of 10, a child should have learnt and mastered at least one skill

No child is too small to learn a skill

9 Volunteering and Gaining Experience Early

Remember that the happiest people are not getting more, but those giving more
- Jackson Brown Junior

It's easier to make a bunch. It's much tougher to make a difference
- Tom Brokaw

Be of service. Whether you make yourself available to a friend or co-worker, or you make time every month to do volunteer work, there is nothing that harvests more of a feeling of empowerment than being of service to someone in need
Gillian Anderson

To volunteer means to freely offer to do something. When someone volunteers, he/she would work for an establishment without being paid for it. It is entirely the person's choice to do so because he/she is not cajoled into it.

It is important for your kids to gain work experience early enough. During holidays, they could maximize their time by volunteering to work. Teach them to volunteer to do small jobs because it will help them gain competence fast. By choosing to work and accepting to volunteer, they will be going beyond the head knowledge into a more practical realm or dimension.

Many kids do not know how to associate with people. They are used to the regular faces they get to see at home and at school so each time they are exposed to a larger environment with more crowd, they tend to have no clue on what to do or how to relate with other people. Volunteering will help them to meet new people and get familiar with different work environments and it will also teach them to relate with people from various backgrounds and walks of life. There are several adults who are desperately in search of jobs who should volunteer to acquire a skill while waiting but are either unwilling or unable to do so and so if the children are exposed to volunteering early enough, they would have an advantage that their counterparts do not have.

A child can volunteer to work in the following places:

1. Libraries
2. Factories
3. Hospitals
4. National parks
5. Museums
6. Retirement and elderly homes
7. Orphanages
8. Restaurants
9. Government establishment
10. Computing centers
11. Barber shops
12. Hair dressing and beauty salon.

Reasons for Volunteering

People volunteer for different purposes. Some of the reasons for doing so include:

1. Enlightenment
2. To learn or acquire a new skill
3. To show kindness or generosity
4. To gain exposure
5. To improve the quality of one's life
6. To build relationships
7. To gain relevant experiences
8. To gain knowledge
9. To give back to the society
10. To fill up missing links

Benefits of Volunteering

1. Skill development
2. Knowledge acquisition
3. Experience
4. Build relationships
5. Improve career prospects
6. Versatility

REFLECTIONS

Volunteering is to the advantage of the child

It exposes the child to many opportunities

Volunteering sets the child up for opportunities

Volunteering can be a rewarding experience

Financial Integrity 10

Real integrity is doing the right thing knowing that nobody is going to know whether you did it or not

- Oprah Winfrey

People of integrity do what they said they are going to do. Others have excuses

-Anonymous

Integrity is telling myself the truth. Honesty is telling the truth to other people

-Spenser Johnson

Integrity is the quality of being honest and maintaining a strong moral principle. The good book says "a good name is better than riches" (prov. 22:1). A lot of people have attained amazing heights but did not develop the necessary qualities that would keep or sustain them up there. Someone said and rightly too that it takes a man many years to build a reputation but just a second to crumble it. After all is said and done, integrity remains a quality your child must hold in high esteem.

Once upon a time, an ageing emperor in the East decided on a novel way to choose his successor. He called the city's youths to his palace. Handing out some special seeds, he told them, "Go and plant these seeds. In a year's time, I will judge your plants and choose the new emperor."One boy named Ling took his pot home and planted the seed. Every day he watered it but nothing grew. Even though his friends at school were talking about their growing plants, Ling only had an empty pot.

When the day came to return to the palace, Ling went with a frightened heart. The emperor appeared. All the other youths had magnificent plants. When the emperor saw Ling's plant, he summoned him to the front and announced to the crowd, "Behold your new emperor! He has courage and integrity because all the seeds I gave you were boiled and useless. He was the only one not to cheat. He will be a wise ruler over you all."Ling refused to compromise despite all that was promised. Out of all who were handed those special seeds, only one person stood out.

Kids need to realize it is never about how many people are doing what or how they are doing it but that the most important thing is, whether it is the right thing, whether it will hurt someone and whether they would be able to defend their actions anywhere anytime?

Many times, the crowd is wrong so kids must concentrate on what is right and not how many persons are doing it because that is the import of integrity. Teach your kids to value a good name more than riches and gold because on the long run, their integrity will speak for them. To do this, tell your kids that:

- Integrity is returning what is in your possession that isn't originally yours
- Integrity is saying the truth at all times
- Integrity is being content with what you have
- Integrity is honesty and having honest intentions
- Integrity is abhorring dishonest intentions
- Integrity is apologizing when one is wrong
- Integrity is being the same person to everyone
- Integrity is detesting dishonest scales

REFLECTIONS

Integrity is priceless. It must be valued above money

Everyone who wants to last in business or any endeavour must be a person of integrity

Dishonesty is a killer of success

Habits Formation

(21 DAYS CHALLENGE)

It is a popular belief that for someone to get used to doing a particular thing, they need to do it consistently for at least 21 days. We have been talking about savings and investment. Let's now take a look at some practical dimensions for children. It will require engaging your child in a 21 day exercise. Throughout these 21 days, you are to assign a particular task to your child (it could be more than one). At the end of the day, you will be required to give him some money for the job done.

Out of what he earns, he is to save 60% from the money for 21 days and then use the remaining 40% to buy whatever he wishes. However, he must be able to assist the family by providing what the family needs. It could be bread, match box, candles, etc. whatever he can afford. The idea is for him to take part in providing for the family for these 21 days while saving and meeting some of his needs.

Take note also that he must keep accurate record of the expenses made because he would need them at the end of the 21days. This is a sample of what I mean, the first being an example:

DAY	INCOME	SAVINGS (60%)	EXPENSES	TOTAL
Day 1	500 naira	300 naira	Match box- 20 naira Biscuit- 10 naira Bread – 150 naira	480 naira
Day 2				
Day 3				
Day 4				
Day 5				

Day 6				
Day 7				
Day 8				
Day 9				
Day 10				
Day 11				
Day 12				
Day 13				
Day 14				
Day 15				
Day 16				
Day 17				
Day 18				
Day 19				
Day 20				

Day 21				
TOTAL				

At the end of the 21days exercise, he is to calculate his savings and then think of where he could invest the money he was able to realize within the period. He is also to calculate his expenses so as to know how much he spent on his wants/needs. There is also a need for an analysis: To determine whether he spent his reserve income wisely; if there were things he bought he could have done without; If it was possible to save more than 60% of his income; and if there were some things he should avoid spending on by the next month.

His ability to honestly answer these questions will affect how he would begin to handle money. As he grows, his understanding of money will continue to broaden and he would grow into a responsible man/woman who understands how money works and will become properly equipped to manage whatever he earns.

THE MILLION DOLLAR KID

The MILLLION DOLLAR KID book was such a delight. I wish I read it when I was a child, either way, it was like a whole new experience.

Afy Douglas
(Music & Life Coach, Plus Life International)

I hesitate to describe this book as a "Kid" book simply because the content will benefit everyone both old and young. Very important truths are all woven around it. Simple but very important topics were covered, this is not just for kids.

Ijay Grigs
(Gilgal Educational)

This is a guide to teenagers and SO MUCH MORE. I wish my parents knew all these, this book changed my perspective.

Darlington
(President Dynamic Teens)

I don't think there's anyone who wouldn't benefit from reading this book. It comes as a reminder to me as a Parent. The lessons in this book is important for any smart parent.

Nancy Iheduru Msc.
(Author, Get Smarter at Parenting, ED CCds)

www.ingramcontent.com/pod-product-compliance
Lightning Source LLC
LaVergne TN
LVHW091111150826
845673LV00002B/775

* 9 7 9 8 8 4 4 3 6 0 1 5 2 *